Presidents' Day

by Meredith Dash

www.abdopublishing.com

Published by Abdo Kids, a division of ABDO, PO Box 398166, Minneapolis, Minnesota 55439.

Copyright © 2015 by Abdo Consulting Group, Inc. International copyrights reserved in all countries. No part of this book may be reproduced in any form without written permission from the publisher.

Printed in the United States of America, North Mankato, Minnesota.

052014

092014

Photo Credits: Corbis, Shutterstock, State Archives of Florida / Florida Memory, Thinkstock © spirit of america p.17 / Shutterstock.com

Production Contributors: Teddy Bworth, Jennie Forsberg, Grace Hansen

Design Contributors: Candice Keimig, Laura Rask, Dorothy Toth

Library of Congress Control Number: 2013952089

Cataloging-in-Publication Data

Dash, Meredith.

 Presidents' Day / Meredith Dash.

   p. cm. -- (National holidays)

ISBN 978-1-62970-046-5 (lib. bdg.)

Includes bibliographical references and index.

1. Presidents' Day--Juvenile literature. 2. Presidents--United States--Juvenile literature.   I. Title.

394.261--dc23

                    2013952089

Table of Contents

Presidents' Day

Presidents' Day began

as Washington's Birthday.

5

It celebrated George Washington. He was the first US president.

It was every 22nd of February.

That is Washington's birthday.

It became a **national holiday** in 1879. President Rutherford B. Hayes signed it into law.

In 1968, the **Uniform Holiday Act** was signed. All **national holidays** moved to Mondays.

13

The holiday's name changed too. It is now called Presidents' Day.

14

Who We Celebrate

We celebrate every US president.

When We Celebrate

We celebrate every

3rd Monday in February.

18

How We Celebrate

It is a **patriotic** day. We remember our great leaders.

20

More Facts

- James Buchanan was the only US president to never marry.

- Beginning with President William H. Taft in 1910, every president has thrown a ceremonial first pitch at a baseball game (except for Jimmy Carter).

- James Madison was the shortest president at 5 feet 4 inches (1.6 m). Abraham Lincoln was the tallest at 6 feet 4 inches (1.9 m).

Glossary

national holiday – also known as a federal holiday, a special event celebrated by a country.

patriotic – loyalty to a country.

Uniform Holiday Act – an act of US Congress that moved all national holidays to Mondays.

Index

abdokids.com

Use this code to log on to abdokids.com and access crafts, games, videos and more!

Abdo Kids Code:
NPK0465